Over-the-Top Animals
Biggest Snake
by Suzane Nguyen
BLASTOFF! Beginners
BLASTOFF! BEGINNERS, AN IMPRINT OF BELLWETHER MEDIA BY FLUTTERBEE

Blastoff! Beginners are developed by literacy experts and educators to meet the needs of early readers. These engaging informational texts support young children as they begin reading about their world. Through simple language and high frequency words paired with crisp, colorful photos, Blastoff! Beginners launch young readers into the universe of independent reading.

Sight Words in This Book

a	big	have	long	these
are	eat	help	on	they
as	find	it	their	with

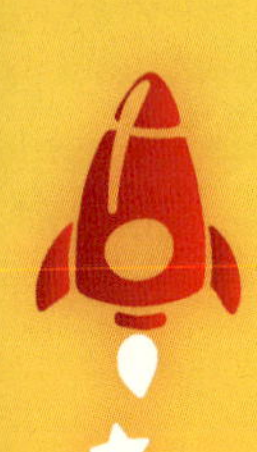

This edition first published in 2027 by Bellwether Media, Inc.

For information regarding permission, write to Bellwether Media, Inc., Attention: Permissions Department, 3500 American Blvd W, Suite 150, Bloomington, MN 55431.

Library of Congress Cataloging-in-Publication Data is available at www.loc.gov or upon request from the publisher.

ISBN: 9798898800055 (hardcover)
ISBN: 9798898801410 (ebook)

Editor: Betsy Rathburn Designer: Laura Sowers

Printed in the United States of America, North Mankato, MN.

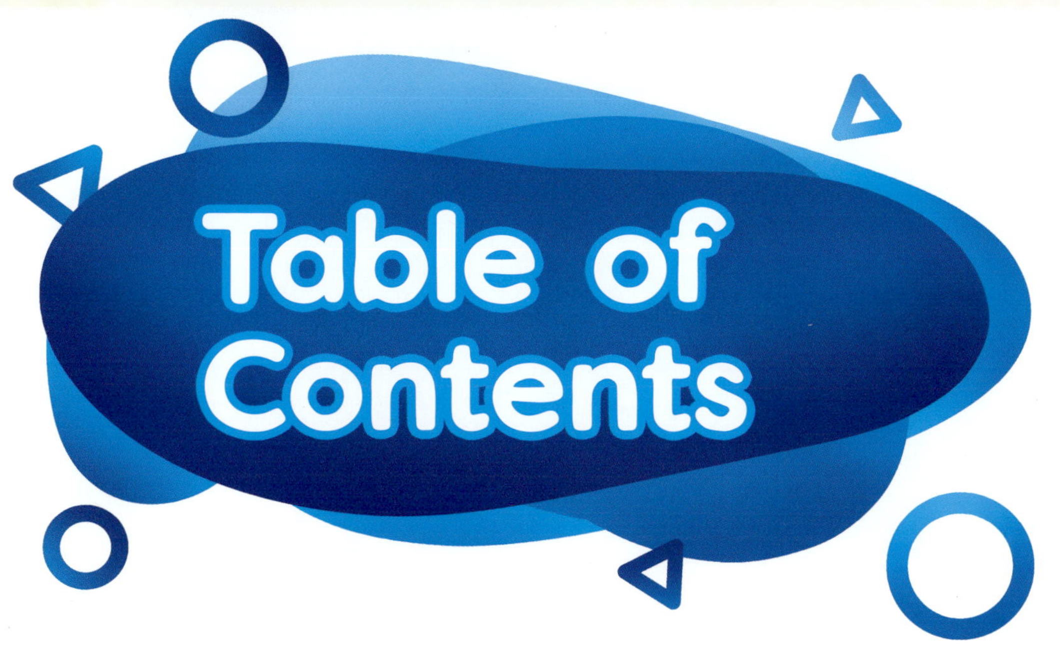
Table of Contents

A green anaconda
found a meal.
It holds on tight!

These snakes are **reptiles**.

They are heavy. They weigh as much as a piano!

They have big mouths. They have tiny teeth.

They have long **forked tongues.**

forked
tongue

Finding Food

They have big **muscles**. They hunt big **prey**.

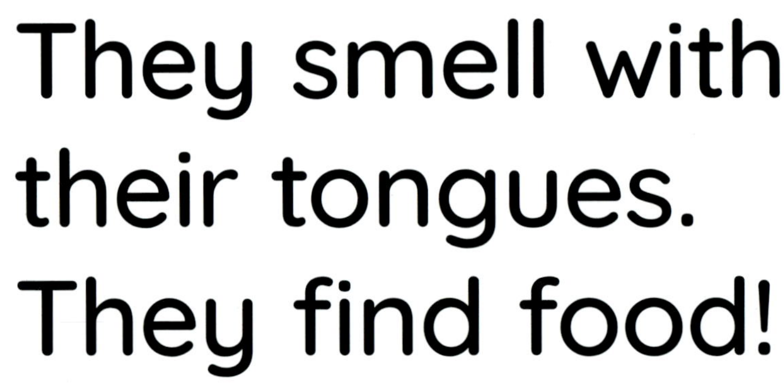

They smell with
their tongues.
They find food!

They open their big mouths. They eat prey whole!

These snakes hunt easily. Their size helps!

The Biggest Snake

Body Parts

Using Their Size

hunt big prey

open mouth wide

eat prey whole

Glossary

forked tongues tongues that are split in two at the tip

muscles body tissues that help move parts of the body

prey animals that are hunted by other animals for food

reptiles cold-blooded animals that lay eggs

To Learn More

ON THE WEB

FACTSURFER

Factsurfer.com gives you a safe, fun way to find more information.

1. Go to www.factsurfer.com.
2. Enter "biggest snake" into the search box and click 🔍.
3. Select your book cover to see a list of related content.

Index

The images in this book are reproduced through the courtesy of: Marigold, front cover; Welington Coelho, pp. 3, 22; Luciano Candisani/ Minden Pictures/ SuperStock, pp. 4-5; Nynke, p. 6; André LABETAA, pp. 6-7, 23 (reptiles); Luis, pp. 8-9; Jenhung Huang, p. 10; Michael Patrick O'Neill/ Alamy Stock Photo, pp. 10-11; M. Watsonantheo/ Mary Evans Picture Library/ Pantheon/ SuperStock, pp. 13-13; Passakorn, p. 14; Minden Pictures/ SuperStock, pp. 14-15; mlharing, pp. 16-17; slowmotiongli, pp. 18-19; Michael Nolan/ Robert Harding Picture Library/ Robert Harding/ SuperStock, pp. 20-21; Vaclav Sebek, p. 22 (hunt big prey); chamleunejai, p. 22 (open mouth wide); Tony Crocetta/ Biosphoto/ SuperStock, p. 22 (eat prey whole); mgkuijpers, p. 23 (forked tongues); Hin255, p. 23 (muscles); Ondrej Prosicky, p. 23 (prey).